DOES THIS MAKE SENSE?

A Jump Start on Your Self-Help Journey

Erin Battle

For London,

It's expected for everyone to say I made you,
but I want you to know that it is you who made me.

I love you, Babydoll.

*You never know how or when you'll have an impact,
or how important your example can be to someone else.*
—Denzel Washington

CONTENTS

Introduction 1

Chapter 1 5
How did I get here?

Chapter 2 14
Big T

Chapter 3 24
Relationships

Chapter 4 36
Oh Baby!

Chapter 5 45
Change

Chapter 6 51
Purpose

Chapter 7 57
Heal

Epilogue 64

Resources 66

Who is Erin Battle? 68

INTRODUCTION

Have you ever just felt stuck to the point where you put your hands over your face and asked yourself, "What the heck am I doing with my life!?" Cool, me too, more than once. I think we just became friends.

No, but seriously . . .

Whether it's dating, careers, parenting, societal pressures, codependent/toxic relationships, or just feeling like you're on the hamster wheel of life; you name it, we've all experienced at least one, a time or two . . . or three. Whatever your vice, there's good energy and peace of mind waiting within arm's reach. But here's the catch: no one can want it more for you, than you.

The thing is, there's only one of you in this whole world, and guess what! You didn't come with an instruction manual or navigation system. That means it is very much okay for you to not know which way to go all the time, or how to maneuver through life to achieve your best possible outcome. That also means it is okay to make right and wrong decisions in order to learn how to operate at your full potential. People never take into consideration that this is our first time doing this thing called life; it's trial and error. The literal meaning of trial and error is the process of experimenting with various methods of doing something until one finds the most successful one.[1] If there's only one you, how can anyone tell YOU that YOU are doing YOU wrong?

There have been great examples of people who attempted to follow the "fool-proof" guidelines to reach success. They thought they could graduate from high school, then college, get a career in their field, and live lavishly with their beautiful home, family, and dog. Instead they ended up in debt, still living at home, and waiting for that one motivational post that will get them into the gym, to quit their job, and to start their own business doing what they love, to make them a fortune. I created the *Erin Battle Method* to speak to people like them. I've been a social worker my whole life, professionally for seven years. Part of my job responsibilities include monitoring children's physical, psychological, and educational well-being. I also team with other agencies, children, and families to meet every family's specific needs. My intentions are always to have the family's dynamic be healthier in bonds and communication by the time of the case closure. Being a

---

1 https://www.lexico.com/en/definition/trial

social worker made me realize that no matter the demographic or financial status, we're all just really trying to figure it out.

Back in the day, before social media, "what you see is what you get" was a well-rounded phrase that held a lot of weight. Ironically with all the visual outlets that social media offers, what you see isn't at all what you get now, the majority of the time. People create the lives they want by controlling the show. There are failures in every success story. From financial struggles to failed business ventures, there's the ugly 'before', and the cringeworthy journey that isn't appealing until after the success. I'm writing this book DURING my questionable journey, which at times has felt like I took a left turn when I should've gone straight. You're reading my book, and I'm here to honestly tell you I still don't have it all figured out.

Maybe I should've said that at the end...

Nonetheless, whenever I am on one of my rants, when I'm done, I have a habit of asking "Does that make sense?" I always want to make sure whoever is on the receiving end of my conversations understands my perspective, and that I always have the best intentions when giving advice. I can only hope that this current part of my journey can assist you with the current part of yours. Welcome to my judgement-free zone. Nothing about your life is anything to be ashamed of, because I can guarantee, whatever it is, you're not the first and you definitely won't be the last to experience it. I'm here to tell you what you already know, which is life can be shitty sometimes; but I believe the best therapy is being able to relate to others and remind yourself that you are not alone. Because honestly . . . everybody shits.

At the end of each chapter, there will be a reflection activity, and additional space for you to write whatever is on your mind or your heart. Use it to your healing advantage. Be open, be vulnerable, be you.

CHAPTER 1

"You can't really know where you are going until
you know where you have been." —Maya Angelou

How did I get here?

In the process of a healing journey, you have to peel back
the layers and reflect on why and where you picked up
some of your best and worst personality traits. When I
knew it was my time to heal, I was not even sure where to
begin. I chose to start with the first bad childhood mem-
ory that I could recall.

Now, we weren't rich, but I was a fairly sheltered child
growing up. I had a tribe behind me, AND if one person
said no, there was someone in the village that would say
yes. It was a gift and a curse. The gift was I lived on Easy
Street, and the curse was coming into my adult life never
knowing any real responsibility. My superhero mom
made sure that my sister and I had everything we wanted.

My dad made sure he could account for every dime of his hard-earned money spent.

My parents separated when I was two years old, and my dad showed up for special events, and maybe weekend lunch dates. It wasn't until I got older that I found out when I turned 13, my mom decided to file child support on my dad, and anyone involved in taking his money from him caught his wrath. Ironically, his wrath turned out to be nothing at all. My dad was not a fan of confrontation, he just wouldn't say anything to you; including me or my sister. No communication, not even birthday calls. I reached out to him, of course, but couldn't understand why he'd never answer. I eventually gave up. But this resentment at such a vital stage in a teenage girl's life couldn't have come at a worse time. The transition into a woman, yet lacking the love from the man who's supposed to love her the most, was devastating.

In middle school and high school, I found myself learning the love languages of men through my classmates. This mixture of things that included what they saw on television, heard from a friend, or on a song demonstrated to me how men were supposed to treat me. My family was full of strong women, and their constant coaching of what not to do was only a guide. My Godmother's relentless biblical background instilled fear in me of burning in hell for the rest of my life, which also played a huge role. However, the lack of love shown from my dad followed me into every intimate and platonic relationship that I had with men. I was not able to recognize the difference between who genuinely cared, and someone who just gave me attention to serve their own purpose. My dad and I reconciled with no explanation of his absence. This shaped my lack of ability to communicate with men, out of fear that if I upset them; like him, they would disappear. I was witnessing my life evolving, but it did not feel like I was making much progress.

College was a very unfamiliar, yet exciting territory. Everyone was much more mature, and for me it was a combination of lax structure, partying, being myself, and still finding myself, all at the same time. I was always the outgoing, funny friend. However, secretly I was insecure and lacking confidence. I let societal pressures turn an amazing personality trait such as my humor into my defense mechanism to counter my insecurities. It wasn't until I was almost done with my undergraduate studies that I realized I had no idea who I was, but had every idea of how I wanted to be perceived. How conflicting, right?

I knew my intentions were never malicious in anything that I did but when you don't know who you are from the inside out, you're constantly working to prove otherwise to the world. You are constantly on the defensive, because your main goal is to alter the perceptions of others to make them see what you want them to see. People I let into my space made me feel ashamed of my college partying days because I did not carry myself as a dated housewife from the '50s. Because I lacked confidence, I would drink to take the edge off. I was having fun and still passing my classes, so yes, I was drinking a lot, but I'd like to tell myself that it was responsibly. I let others' idea of who I was supposed to be and what I was supposed to act like dictate the level of shame I had for myself.

The formula for a miserable, unfulfilled life is letting societal norms mandate why, when, what, and how you are supposed to leave your stamp on the world. This brought about a period in my life where I felt like not only did no one understand what I was going through, but I also had no one that I trusted enough to talk to about how I was ashamed that I was seen as the drunken party girl. So, I took a trip. There's this little place called Rock Bottom, just South of Wits' End, and boy, was it unpleasant. Reflecting made me realize that rock bottom can be visited more than once and looks different depending on the stage you are at in your life. The more you have to lose, the more expensive that Rock Bottom trip costs. Depression is real, and does not discriminate with any age or situation. As small as it seems today, that time in my life hit me hard. I felt alone, I alienated myself, and was no longer the fun friend. It was true what they said about being so low, the only way to look is up.

Consequently, during that shift in my life, it introduced me to Self. Self then introduced me to Self-Care, Self-Help, and most importantly, Self-Love. I became closer to God, and no, this is not a religious book, but know that God (or whatever you choose to call Her) exists with or without organized religion. I started reading more self-help books, which I used to think were nothing but pages of pity during my "*The Coldest Winter Ever* by Sister Souljah" days. I had a few major setbacks along the way, but I came back better than ever. My focus was different and so was my confidence. I felt great so I stopped the reading and healing work; I thought I was done healing.

Now that I thought I knew how to prioritize my Self, the new and improved me was back, partying again. Not as hard, because I was older, and my recovery time wasn't what it used to be. I set my goals, got a second job because I was ready to buy a house and wanted to speed up the process. I met and dated my daughter's dad. We had fun, our relationship was not the healthiest, but I fell in love with his potential. With so many failed relationships under my belt, I had a new strategy. I purposely did not look for someone who could reciprocate all that I had to offer, because he would have no choice but to look at me as a prize. I figured that whoever I dated would be convinced that he'd be an idiot to lie or cheat having a beautiful, ambitious, diamond in the rough like me for a girlfriend. HA! What a dumb-ass strategy!

Let me just tell you, THAT didn't work either. That wasn't confidence, that was actually the complete opposite. I then became pregnant with the most precious little girl, who I now know is my biggest blessing. I went through a roller coaster of emotions during my first year of being a new mom. I later promised myself that with any serious decision I made, I'd give myself the same advice that I'd give my daughter; nothing more, nothing less. It wasn't until I knew I had to protect my baby at all costs, that I had to change my standards. My daughter pushed me back to my self-love journey. I still wasn't where I needed to be, but I knew I had to be better for her. Because no matter what, I refused to be the reason she lowered her standards to be the prize. She was going to know without a doubt that she was the prize, no matter what.

Mentally, I was not ready to return to my career as a social worker after my maternity leave, but it was time. I never knew how to separate my personal life from my work, because I vowed to never ONLY be a policy-pushing social worker. My families would know I was one of the good ones, and that I really cared. I started to have a deeper connection with some of the parents on my cases when I heard their stories, because just like me they lacked self-love. I spoke to the children on my cases differently. They needed to hear that they were worthy and loved, even if I was the only person to tell them. Some of my families saved me, and had no idea they were helping me just as much as I was helping them. I often struggled with my families not being receptive to my help. Although my intentions were good, this was me selfishly rushing their process. No one is going to change on your time, they're only going to change on theirs.

You can never stop learning, because you are constantly evolving with every new experience you encounter.

Some things may not make sense in the moment, but I have learned to trust my process. With the necessary work that I continue to do on myself, I have come to the conclusion that no one can give the world what I can give the world, because there's only one me. Just like you, friend, there's no possible way that I can do ME the wrong way. How can anyone tell you you're not perfect, when there's only one you? This means we can only perfect our perfectness. So, if I've gotten you to read this far, it means that everything that I've been through, led me to you. All of the work I've done on myself, and all of the books that I've read thus far, not only guided my journey to help myself, but to have the opportunity to help you as well. Think of this read as a talk with your friend. I really appreciate you for letting me into your personal space, all while I let you into mine.

Reflection: Let's start with me giving you a standing ovation for being here, reading to perfect your perfectness. How did you get here? Where are you trying to go?

CHAPTER 2

"Not everything that is faced can be changed,
but nothing can be changed until it is faced."
—James Baldwin

Big T

Who is Big T, you ask? None other than your old pal, Trauma.

Trauma wears many different faces. Off the top of my head, some examples of where trauma could have come from are: emotional and physical abuse or neglect, sexual abuse, bullying, addiction, accidental bodily harm, heartbreak, chronic illness, death...we can literally go on forever. Something as big as rape, or something as small as stubbing your toe, can cause trauma in your life. Considering everyone's level of tolerance is subjective; trauma does not discriminate either. Another very important thing to know about the Big T is that the trauma itself does not have to happen directly to you. There's another case of trauma, called vicarious trauma. Meet Little T. Vicarious Trauma, or Little T, is a secondary trauma that one can encounter by witnessing someone else's traumatic experience, or merely just hearing about it.[2]

Trauma is like a chameleon. Its skin changes colors in response to its emotions, such as anger or fear, changes in light, temperature or humidity.[3] Like a chameleon, trauma camouflages itself so it is not recognizable in its regular environment. If left untreated, trauma is continuously ignited by triggers, and will constantly remind your conscious or subconscious of an undesirable yet familiar place.

Let's talk about Big T . . .

When I was fifteen years old, I was homeschooled; and while everyone in my house was at work, I'd stay home and work on my weekly curriculum packets. I was a sophomore in high school, and I had a younger neighbor who we'll call Kevin. He was like a little brother, and he would do his homework with me every day after school. It was our regular routine, so regular that I would leave my door unlocked and he'd come right in like clockwork, Monday through Friday. One particular day I was sitting at the dining room table and I heard my door open earlier than usual, and it wasn't Kevin. It was Kevin's stepdad; we'll call him Bozo. Bozo walked in and I asked him what

---

2 https://www.livescience.com/amp/51061-chameleon.html

3 https://www.counseling.org/docs/trauma-disaster/fact-sheet-9---vicarious-trauma.pdf

he was doing there, my heart beating fast and my voice kind of trembling. Bozo was likely in his late 40s, built like Melvin from the movie *Baby Boy*, and needless to say, I was terrified.

He walked over to me, and turned my chair to face him. I asked him what he was doing, and he said, "Shut up, girl," in the least aggressive tone, and locked my wrists to the arm rests of the chair with his hands. I was frozen at this point. I couldn't move, couldn't talk, couldn't scream, and couldn't fight. He used his right knee to open my legs and took my right wrist and placed it with the left one to lock them down together in order to free up one of his hands. He unbuttoned my pants with his right hand and rubbed my "private area" while he forced his tongue in my mouth while tears just ran down my face. He stopped after about a minute, turned around, and just walked out and closed the door behind him. He didn't say a word and just left me there in the chair, violated. After a couple minutes, I bolted to the door, locked every lock, and sat there on the floor with my back to the door crying.

The turning of my locked door knob startled me and snapped me out of the daze I didn't know I was in. I looked through the peephole and it was Kevin cursing at me for locking him out. I let him in and he immediately asked me what was wrong after seeing my red eyes and wet face. I was silent because I couldn't tell him what happened; it was all my fault. I should've done something to stop it, and I didn't. He asked repeatedly and I finally broke down and told him. He said he was going to call his mom and I begged him not to. He told me I was crazy and called her anyway. She asked to speak to me and I shook my head no, but he pushed the phone into my hands.

Hello?

Kevin's mom: Did he touch you and kiss you?

Me: Yes.

Kevin's mom: Did he kiss you hard?

Assuming that meant with tongue, I agreed.

Kevin's mom: Don't tell anyone and don't call the police because he'll get in a lot of trouble.

She had just confirmed everything I was thinking. I couldn't tell anyone. He'd go to jail, lose his family, and I'd be the one responsible for it all. After I hung up Kevin asked me what she said, and I told him.

Kevin: What! You have to call your mom. Call her now!

After we argued for about a minute, I called my mom. I told her everything that happened, including what Kevin's mom advised.

*Mom: Are you kidding me!? F**k that b**ch! Lock the doors and don't answer it unless it's the police, I'm on my way home!*

Kevin's phone rang, he answered and handed the phone to me again. It was Bozo, he said *"Girl, what are you doing!? I was just playing with you."*

I hung up.

When the police arrived, I remember there being so many of them. There were several different officers who repeatedly asked me to tell them the story over again. This probably was the second most traumatizing thing about this whole situation. After I'd had enough, I cried and said I didn't want to talk to anyone else and locked myself in the room.

The next day my mom made me pack up some clothes and sent me to live with my aunt, about forty-five minutes away from home, until she could figure some things out. No less than a month later, my mom told us we were relocating about ten minutes away from my aunt. I had to move away from my friends, and had to finish high school with strangers in a predominantly white community where I was now the minority. I was devastated. I blamed myself for years because of what I could've done differently to stop all that from happening to me.

In the previous chapter, I briefly discussed my relationship with my dad. If I were to elaborate, I'd say I struggled with our relationship his entire life. Again, he was not an emotional person, yet my maternal family was very affectionate. I grew up with hugs and kisses at greetings and goodbyes. My dad's tone was always uncomfortable and rushed when he said "I love you too," before he hung up with me on the phone. Despite his lack of affection, I LOVED my daddy more than anything and all I wanted was to be sure enough that he felt the same way. No matter how much love my mom showed me, it was my dad's enthusiasm I was looking for whenever I accomplished anything. Not at all because I didn't love my mom just as much, but because I could never tell if my dad even cared. He wasn't easily impressed.

I was a spoiled nineteen-year-old who thought I had it all figured out, and I would call my dad after an argument with my mom. My dad's advice would go something like this, "You just need to move out and start living on your own. When I was your age, I had left home and bought my own car." Move out? Yeah, right! Fast-forward years later to my college graduation on June 14th. I finally did it, and my whole family was there to see me cross the stage, including my dad. After the ceremony was over, I called him to find him in the crowd, because I was so excited and felt so accomplished. He answered and said he had left, and was upset that after crossing the stage I didn't come and greet him. I explained that the ceremony wasn't over, and I couldn't just leave before they released us. I was heartbroken, angry, and fed up. I didn't speak to him for the next seven months. Then, on January 24th, I received a call from my Aunt Linda, his younger sister, asking me about my dad passing away that morning.

This was so surreal. The dynamic of our relationship was to not talk while we were upset, and pick back up when we were ready. Well, I was ready now, but it was too late. I've experienced loss before, but grieving seems different when it's a parent. I was not only experiencing loss, I actually felt lost. I hadn't completed the mission of figuring myself out, and now a third of the puzzle pieces were gone. I also was never able to restore our relationship back to where I wanted it to be. I had no children at the time, so he didn't even get the chance to prove himself as super grandpa to make up for his role as a distant dad.

So now, we're not just talking about childhood trauma, let's add in adulthood trauma; both unresolved. Neither of the people involved in these situations were able to contribute to my healing and give me back what they robbed me of. I had to get it back on my own. So, before I was introduced to therapy, or talked to anyone for that matter, I started to write. I wrote letters to Bozo telling him how disgusting he was and how him taking advantage of me made him a clown. I wrote letters to my dad about my resentment, sadness, and even my accomplishments. I did things that made me happy and I cried a whole lot. However, in my continuous healing journey, there's a couple of very important things that I've learned along the way . . .

1. You'll never be able to fully heal from anything you continue to claim victim over. What I mean by this is, there is the perspective that you are still a victim of your trauma. However, there's an alternative perspective that you refusing to let your trauma hinder your growth makes you a survivor.

2. Everyone has a story; sometimes you just need help making it make sense. Suppressing your emotions and feelings is a sure way to drive yourself

crazy. No matter how you believe your story will be received, it needs to be told. The fact that you're here to tell it speaks volumes. Tell it at your own pace. Start journaling about it, research and read about similar success stories, and talk about it when you're ready. But whatever you do, don't hold it in. You never know whose story *you* can help make sense of.

There are signs that we are dealing with unresolved trauma, and I am not referring to your zodiac sign. Please stop blaming all your toxic personality traits on your zodiac sign. However, one of the biggest signs that you're dealing with unresolved trauma is that certain situations or places ignite bad memories and emotions. You may get defensive when someone close to you offers advice or constructive criticism. Learn to recognize when someone who cares about you has good intentions when offering alternative solutions for your mental or physical well-being. It's not always an attack on your character, and if you don't know how to respond, just kindly say, "Thank you." Also, I am well aware there are people in your life who seemed to have misplaced all their mirrors, but make it a point to tell you about all your flaws. Try not to totally tune them out. Consider their acknowledgements, thank them, and most importantly, add them to your prayers.

Reflection: What are your stories behind your scars? What Big T are you afraid to face?

CHAPTER 3

"The greatness of a man is not in how much wealth he acquires, but in his integrity and his ability to affect those around him positively."—Bob Marley

Relationships

Big T finds the most satisfaction in relationships, whether they are intimate or platonic. However, I wouldn't be doing relationships any justice if I didn't dedicate a whole chapter to them, so let's talk about it.

A significant thing I have learned is that you cannot expect others to react, reciprocate, or respond the way you would, in any situation. No matter what type of relationship you find yourself in, it is necessary for you to communicate efficiently enough to be understood, without having to be figured out. You have to learn to listen to understand, not just to respond. When we're talking about relationships, I'm talking about them all. These include those with your family, friends, intimate partner(s), professional colleagues, and even with yourself. For clarifying purposes, we'll address them individually.

Family

Whether you want to be just like your parent(s) or nothing like them at all, we can agree that their choices and personality traits are what shaped you into the person you are today. If you don't agree, fine, but it's true regardless. How you were raised, whether it was pleasant or unpleasant, plays a huge role in your life decisions and how you're raising your children, if you have them. Like I've said before, I had a village: my amazing mother, my kindhearted grandma, my overly resilient Godmother, and other family and kin. However, as the world evolves, I have come to realize that if I were them today, I would've done some things differently, handled some situations with more care, and been more attentive on some occasions.

More times than not, they did the best they could with what they knew at the time. But then there's certain situations where you realize many of your elders are stuck in their ways, and pretty much done working on or trying to find themselves. They've found as much as they could and called off the search. For example, millennials are far more open to therapy and mental health services. We are into holistic healing, daily mantras, and positive vibes. I always say, if some days are so bad you even have to sage the sage. Nonetheless, we're open. I've found that many encounters I have with the older generations show they were taught to be strong and push through it, which in turn forces them to keep Big T close.

Suppressing traumatic experiences that they encountered in their households and in their lives as children to adulthood, some have mastered blocking things out. I am sure this has much to do with the arguments I had with my mom and dad on several occasions, where we just couldn't see eye to eye. One lesson I've learned is that with any disagreement, you can NEVER force your perspective on another person, especially one who's been here longer and seen more than you in their lifetime. Respect each other's opinions, and understand that no matter how unreasonable that parent or child may come off, you cannot see the world through someone else's eyes.

How about relatives, not the ones who support and encourage you, the ones who manage to clear the room of positivity or need a favor with every phone call or visit? Can you not pay a visit or check in on a relative without them gossiping? Can you trust them and count on them to do the right thing when you're not around? Do you have relatives that have what seems like an unlimited amount of favors to ask? I do highly encourage you to address certain things privately with the relative(s) in question. However, if you've tried that method and they don't respect your space, exit stage left.

Many of you may even have relatives who also play the role of your past or even current abuser. I do suggest you seek healing from another source first. Then, if or when you're ready you can revisit, but you do not owe anyone your peace. If my daddy taught me anything, he taught me that nobody's safe when it comes to your peace of mind. Stop allowing yourself to be manipulated into thinking that just being related to someone gives them the right to steal your joy. Stop feeling obligated to attend family gatherings with anyone who regresses your healing. Family is not just who you share blood with, but who you'd shed blood for.

Friendships

It used to be so simple; the person who always shared their snack with you at school was the most loyal. I've grown to understand the filter system between best friends, close friends, people you know, and leeches. The filter system is necessary, because again, you should always be conscious of who you allow in your space. I'm the best friend that doesn't allow my best friend to be best friends with anyone else. She can have as many close friends as she wants but after twenty-eight years of blood, sweat, and tears . . . we ride together, we die together; bad moms for life. But let's get into the meaning of friend. My personal definition of a friend is someone who is genuine, has your best interest at all times, and whose character and integrity are never in question. A friend is never intentionally going to make you feel ashamed for something that they don't agree with. Friends also don't confuse judgment for advice. A friend is going to be happy to support your accomplishments no matter the progress of their success.

Over the years, I've built relationships with the most loving, positive, encouraging, and inspiring people who became closer to me than any blood relation could be. I don't even call those my close friends, those are my "framily" members.

People who you know—it could be mutual friends, old classmates, old coworkers, the list goes on—these are people you see in passing, or even text from time to time about things that may be beneficial to you or them. As a good person, never withhold anything that you know could be beneficial to another person. No matter the illusion of social media, life is not a competition, and you should always be willing to share your resources.

Now for the leeches, the people who just take, take, and take some more. They serve you no purpose and are only around for their benefit. They may drain you of energy, and tend to overstay their welcome. They don't encourage your growth, but actually hinder it. These are people who you pay for their company. Whether you're paying with money, food, drugs, alcohol, sex, or your time, these people have to go. Because if you don't let them go, you're just as much of a leech to them as they are to you.

Intimate Partner

I know everyone thinks they can write a book on all the things they've been through in relationships, but listen to me...I'm your girl. Let me tell you what my biggest problem was: if I met a guy I really liked and we did relationship stuff, in my mind, we were in a relationship. I literally was just waiting for him to propose to me at that point. This was all fun and games until special occasions came up and my expectations were never met. I never demanded anything, just settled for whatever they were willing to give me.

This turned into me being reluctant to tell them what I wanted out of the relationship, out of fear that I'd lose it all. I was always under the impression that laying down the lines of what I was expecting out of the relationship early on was me being overbearing and desperate. I never could gauge the right time, and before I knew it, the lines had become so blurred that I lost all sight of what lane I was in. Say what you want, and mean what you say. No one should be intimidated by your expressing what you're looking for in a partner. It is your responsibility to set your own boundaries, and that is up to the other person to decide if they're willing to move forward with anything more than a conversation.

Men, I know you've been waiting to hear a woman say this. Women can be toxic too! I have to admit I've been the toxic one a time or two...or three. I can never give a thorough definition of what it means to be toxic, but it's like being a counterproductive casserole with the main ingredients being manipulation, narcissism, mental and/or physical abuse, with the only consistent aspect being inconsistency. Sometimes we get so used to the dysfunction that we believe that's just the dynamic of the relationship. There's a fine line between dysfunction and incompatibility. Sometimes you're trying to fit the circle block into the square space. No matter how you flip it, unless you change the shape of that circle, it's not going to work. Especially if the sex is great, overlooking red flags can be a breeze.

Understand that intimacy has more depth than just physical pleasure. There are no ties that you have to anyone, including children, that justify staying in a mentally or physically abusive relationship. Falling in love with potential can also be a big problem. The idea that someone can see everything you bring to the table and thinking you can eventually transform that person into the person you want them to be is an illusion. You can never change a person; that person has to be ready to change on their own.

Your partner should always have your best interest at heart, even when you don't agree with each other. Make common priorities just as important as common interests. You have to make sure your goals are aligned and be willing to compromise the order of the goals if necessary. Do you both want children, to get married, to start a business, or to own property? You can both love the same genre of movies, but if investing money is your thing and spending it is theirs, the volcano will erupt sooner than later. Timing is everything. Maybe you haven't devoted enough time to yourself to share *you* with anyone yet. You have to love yourself so much single, that the love you'll have for the person who matches your energy will be effortless. What is meant for you will always be for you.

Professional

I am a black woman who has worked in a professional setting for the bulk of my adult life. My field of choice, social services, brings a diverse crowd in and out of the office. This results in a melting pot of cultural perspectives being brought into your space, whether you agree or not. I have a golden rule about the two types of conversations in the office that I will rarely partake in: religion and politics. Fortunately, no one can tell me about my God, and politics has never been my favorite thing to talk about anyway.

As a black woman, everything from my hair, to my body type, to my dietary preference, can be a conversation for people who get too comfortable. However, you can't avoid ignorance, and sometimes you have to step in and set your boundaries in a respectful manner. If you work with great people with great personalities, you're winning. If you work in a high-stress position like I do, you might have colleagues who, rightfully so, have bad days and can take it out on whoever crosses their path. Some of them might actually hate their job, or their life outside of work. Either way, that's not your problem, it's theirs, and never forget it. Don't allow anyone to make their misery, your misery. Make sure you remain respectful, empathetic, and never give someone a reason to identify you as the problem.

Choose your battles wisely. But if there comes a time when it is absolutely necessary to send a "Per our last conversation" email, I'm here for it; just make sure it's tasteful and you spell check.

Self

If YOU can't make YOU happy, the happiness you receive from someone else will be temporary. If you don't feel love unless someone else is providing the love, your feeling of wholeness is not authentic. YOU have to get to a place where you're okay with things not working. When you get to a point where you're content with your good intentions, you'll be comfortable with people and situations just not being for you. You're literally one of a kind, which means you're irreplaceable. Don't ever let anyone make you believe otherwise.

The people that you allow in your space, I believe, is one of the most important decisions you have to make as a human being. It is more than okay to be selfish with your peace of mind. You don't have to make up excuses or owe anyone an explanation when it's a decision that you had to make for yourself. It is vital that a child is taught to not be easily influenced. You can do this by building their confidence and teaching them to think for themselves. As an adult, you never want to remain in the company of people who have nothing to lose. By nothing to lose, I'm not referring to material things. I'm referring to their career, their business, their children, their dignity, and their freedom. I cannot express this enough, but for the people in the back, make sure you spend time with people who respect, motivate, and encourage your growth. Recognize when something is just not good enough for you and be confident enough to advocate for yourself and say so. Be overly protective of your energy as well as who you allow in your space. Two things you have full control over in this world are your peace of mind and your free time. Treat them like you'll never get them back.

Reflection: What relationships in your life stand out the most, and why? How do you speak to yourself?

CHAPTER 4

"Magic lies in challenging what seems impossible."
—Carol Moseley Braun

Oh Baby!

First let me say this, becoming a mother was the best thing that has ever happened to me in my entire life. Although at the beginning it was the scariest, my daughter forced me to mature in the best way possible. When a parent tries to explain to you the love they have for their child and they light up and can't even put the feeling into words, it's really that deep. Sometimes they even say something like, "I would swim in a pool of flesh-eating piranhas for my baby," I'm here to tell you that's only true three hundred forty-seven days out of the year. I'm also here to tell you about the remaining eighteen days, you think about packing up all your stuff, driving away from that filthy house and the dinner you just burned to soot, and leaving it in

God's hands. I'm laughing writing this, because eighteen days is generous.

Next, I want to say to my mothers who carried those blessings that if no one understands you, I DO. I get that you experience a point of not knowing who you are anymore. Whether you experience that stage during pregnancy or after giving birth, let me tell you who you are: A FREAKING WARRIOR! The woman's body and brain, please let's not forget the brain, go through *so* much during pregnancy, and after giving birth. No matter how a woman looks on the outside, it is biologically proven that after delivery, a woman just doesn't "snap back" to who she was pre-baby. Her hormones are scrambling around like roaches when someone turns on a light. BEAR WITH HER. She's learning herself as a new woman all while having to be a new mom. It's TOUGH!

Postpartum Depression is also a real thing. I did not take on the happiness of having a child until my daughter was four-months-old. It was like there was a baby there, that I knew had to be cared for, but it wasn't mine. The media portrays the aftereffects of childbearing to be glorious for everyone, and that there's an immediate attachment. Moms, you're not alone if you did not feel that instant unconditional love, and you'll be okay. However, don't ignore these feelings and just wait to feel better again. Talk to a professional or join a support group to help you with your superpowers that I absolutely know you have.

Relationships can also get tested, and sometimes it is a big test. Although these are trying times, the character and integrity of a person, especially your partner, should never waver. I've been a single mother since my daughter was six months old. Her father and I broke up after I found out my daughter had a one-month-old brother. Yes, you read that correctly. I said we're friends right, let's talk about it!

I was blindsided by his cheating, let alone bringing another child into the world. I went through a deep depression, on top of my postpartum depression, so serious that I even asked my mother and sister to care for my daughter from that point on because I saw no light at the end of the tunnel. Welcome back to Rock Bottom. My mom told me to shake it off and be strong because my daughter needed me to be strong for her. As great as that sounds, it wasn't that easy. But with therapy and my mother's and sister's support and attentiveness, I made it through. I thank God for them. The scariest thing for me as a first-time mother was doing it all by myself. I already got pregnant out of wedlock and now people will find out that not only did he cheat on me, but had ANOTHER baby while we were together too! Like seriously, how much more could I fail in this relationship?

So, let's pause right here. Do any of you see the biggest problem in all this? The "traditional" way society expects life to go, mine did not. Therefore, I felt like a failure and expected people to look at me as such. Another big problem was that I blamed myself for the actions of another person. No level of blame or manipulation justifies any physical or emotional maltreatment toward you. You cannot make a person be disrespectful, dishonest, physically or emotionally abusive, or unreliable. Repeat after me, I will NOT and CANNOT take responsibility for the actions of another person.

Nonetheless, I went down a rabbit hole of shame and figured my life was pretty much how it was going to be. It was just me and the kid. After some sessions of therapy, I was made aware that the only reason there is a term called "single parent" is because there were some before me and there will be some after me. I presumed that's what my life would be, because who would want me with a kid? After a few more sessions of therapy, another term that surfaced was "step-parent". You would think these wouldn't be Eureka! moments for me, but they were. Listen, when you choose to sit in the darkness, there is no brighter side.

In a conversation I had with a friend, we talked about the expectations of a ***person*** transitioning to a ***parent***. Regardless of where a person is currently at in their life, they are expected to become this role model for their child. In the course of a birth date, it is predicted that a person will provide that child with unconditional love, encouragement, teachings of how to love themselves and others, financial literacy and responsibility, how to be ambitious, and a number of other subjective gender roles. We all know how to do these things, right?

Wrong, again.

Ideally, we'd all like to be prepared mentally, physically, and financially when we bring these precious little gems into the world, but that's not always the case. Many times, we have children with people who are struggling to love themselves, let alone us, but the predictions are that they know how to provide unconditional love to that baby. There are also the parents who project their spitefulness onto their children, because their relationship did not work out and the other parent failed to live up to their expectations. Trauma and brokenness prey on children. What I mean by this, as we all know, is that it is a cycle. Learn to be accountable for the role you play in your own trauma. Understand that accountability is not taking the responsibility for any trauma that you've endured, it's taking a stand and not allowing that trauma to hinder you from being your best self for yourself, and for the people in your life; especially those precious gems.

So many unwritten rules and things you find out by mistake when you become a parent. Being a parent is fulfilling BUT IT'S HARD, Y'ALL! *That Baby Alive* didn't do this parenting thing ANY justice. If we can all agree that parenting isn't the easiest math equation in the book, let's get into something else...

Parent Shaming

Parents, please refrain from forcing your beliefs of how parenting should go on anyone outside of the people that you parent, or don't parent for that matter. How ironic is this, coming from a social worker. This may also be one of the reasons why most of my families loved me so much. I am the social worker that lets my clients know that I too am a parent who gets overwhelmed, frustrated with my child, and has left a diaper on far longer than I should have a time or two...or three.

Note: I am not referring, of course, to anything or anyone that may compromise the safety and/or well-being of any child. The abuse or neglect of an innocent child is intolerable, and resources will be added to the end of this book for any assistance you or anyone you know may need.

However, I am talking about those people who say you should have breastfed instead of using formula, that a mother is damaging their child somehow by breastfeeding him or her too long, that if you feed your kids the same thing every single day, or let a toddler play on a tablet longer than their liking is guilty of child abuse or neglect. Maybe she couldn't breastfeed, or maybe that same meal is the only thing that parent can get that child to eat, or what if that child is learning to read on that tablet? Perspective is everything.

Parent shaming comes in several different forms. In my opinion, parent shaming also includes asking someone why they're not a parent yet. STOP! You don't know that person's story, nor do they owe you an explanation. There are so many variations of upbringing, with added fortunate or unfortunate experiences, that lead us to make the decisions we make when it comes to our own lives and children. I also want to make something clear, whether you have one child, or several children: as long as you continue to experience a child's individual self and what lifestyle or experience they bring into your life, you NEVER stop learning how to be a parent. With every new stage your child enters, it's like a new level of a video game that you have yet to conquer. You know how frustrated you can get when it's taking you longer to master certain levels... my sentiments exactly. Try not to discipline by instilling fear; instead practice patience and be elaborate in your explanations. Don't be so hard on yourself. Like our parents, we're doing the best we can with what we know.

Parents,

To my mothers and fathers who are actively playing a positive role in the life of a child, Godchild, relative, adopted child, foster child, student, neighbor, customer, passenger on your bus, the neighbor's kid who keeps riding their bike on your grass, or even the child in front of the grocery store selling candy for the mysterious fundraiser...from the super social worker herself, thank you from the very bottom of my heart. You guys really rule this world.

Reflection: How was your relationship with your parent(s)? What are some things you would do differently than your parent(s), and why?

CHAPTER 5

"There's always something to suggest that you'll
never be who you wanted to be. Your choice is to take it
or keep on moving."—Phylicia Rashad

Change

In the field of social work, we use a term called the cookie-cutter approach to describe what not to do with the families on our caseloads. If you describe something as having a cookie-cutter approach or style, you mean that the same approach or style is always used and not enough attention is paid to individual differences. In this case I'm referring to some of you and your individual differences, and the same style or approach you continue to use.

Many of us have experienced stages in our lives in which we learned that we don't really know ourselves. Some never realize that they are continuously trying to convince themselves that they are who they say they are. Society can make you believe that you like something because you're supposed to, not because you actually do. Have you ever felt like you were in an unfamiliar space, while in an environment you know well? These are life shifts. When your world just doesn't feel aligned, that's because it's probably not.

Life will make you uncomfortable when it is ready for something different. I understand we don't always know how to navigate this, but don't be afraid of change when you find that your mental, physical, or spiritual self is uncomfortable. When you are physically uncomfortable, you reposition your body to align with your personal level of comfort. When your life feels out of sorts, repositioning is needed to feel aligned with your personal level of growth. When plants outgrow their pots, they are repotted. They are removed from a pot that once fit them perfectly because they've outgrown that space. Your life is no different. You can outgrow people, careers, and even beliefs. Some things are seasonal, and when you reach the end of something, that only means there's a new beginning of something else coming. Change should not be feared, it should be welcomed, as it brings about growth.

When I worked for an insurance company, my salary was well above average, and I knew my job well. Was my lifelong dream to work in insurance? Absolutely not. Was making an above average salary living in Los Angeles the goal? Absolutely. The company was so prominent, job stability was secure and the positions I could be promoted to were endless. It was a great opportunity, but I was miserable. Like my dad said, social work didn't make any money, I was six months pregnant at the time, and the social worker position I was offered would cost me almost a $10,000 annual salary reduction. So, what did I do? That's right, I tossed that offer letter. $10,000? I'm trying to save the world and they want to take $10,000 from me? The nerve. The following Monday came after a refreshing weekend. I sat down at my desk, turned my computer on, and looked at my workload. I exited out of that web application, opened Microsoft Word, and wrote my letter of resignation advising that same day was going to be my last. I walked it into my boss's office and left early. I did one of those laughs that transitions into a cry in the car because, what did I just do!? I made a sacrifice, and it turned into one of the best decisions I've ever made in my life.

Some people find it easier to continue in an uncomfortable environment because it's familiar. You know its highs and you know its lows. You've actually mastered maneuvering through the lows until the highs resurface. Don't get comfortable in your complacency. You have control over your happiness, and if you don't, we've just identified what needs to change first. You're only procrastinating being where you want to be because you're scared to, don't know how to, or don't know where to start the transition. Everything you want could be on the other side of change. The outcome is such a great investment, that the risk you're taking for happiness, peace of mind, and fulfillment, is so worth it. Be responsible, but be determined. Happiness might be your biggest fight, but I can guarantee it will be your most blissful victory.

Don't overthink your change. Your change is individual and specific to your life. You can choose to start with your mindset, and striving to find the brighter side to every situation. You can choose to change your eating habits, and start to be more active. You can even choose to put yourself on a strict budget, to get you one step closer to that home you want to buy. Whatever you need to do to put yourself closer to where you want to be is ultimately your choice, and a sacrifice for your own greater good. When you feel good on the inside, it is projected through everything you do. I heard food even tastes better when the cook is happy. There are also going to be circumstances where you'll lose friends because your growth does not complement their complacency. If your physical and mental wellness is your priority, your actions will be welcomed with open arms by those who are rooting for you. The bottom line is, never be afraid of losing yourself if your current self is still trying to find your best self.

Reflection: Is there anything you want to change in your life? Why or why not? What do you need to do to execute your change? Who can you trust to hold you accountable?

CHAPTER 6

"If you're not making someone else's life better, then you are wasting your time. Your life will become better by making other people's lives better."—Will Smith

Purpose

I believe the common misconception with finding your purpose is that it's all about your personal fulfillment, not about what you can give back to the world and who you can inspire in the process. It's really an equal combination of all three. Your purpose isn't this individual unique thing that you have to conquer *Legends of the Hidden Temple* to find out. YOU are the individual unique thing that makes your purpose your individual unique contribution. I believe everyone's purpose is what they contribute to the greater good of humanity, not because it makes them rich or popular, but because it makes them feel fulfilled and can inspire someone else to do the same.

So again, I've always been the funny friend. It's debatable whether or not I'm the funniest, but I know I'm ranked high on the list. Growing up, that was the way I helped people: by making them laugh. I loved to make people happy, but I did it because it made me feel good. I always knew I wanted to help people, but I never knew what demographic or what kind of help. When I was preparing to go to college, my dad asked me what I was majoring in and I told him Social Work, and boy, did he give me an earful. "Social Work!? That doesn't make any money, and it's one of the most stressful jobs you can have! You need to get into the medical field, if not a doctor, a nurse. Nurses make great money, look into some nursing programs. Let that Social Work thing go."

Guess what I did next? Of course! I changed my major on my college applications and got accepted to start a nursing program in the fall. Anything to make my daddy proud, because I knew my mom would be proud either way. Anyone who knew me knew I was repulsed by people's bare feet touching me. The smell of throw up made me dry heave, I almost fainted every time I saw a needle, and let's not even talk about bad hygiene or human waste. What was I thinking!? I wasn't. I finished one semester of that nursing program and walked straight into the advisor's office and changed my major back to Social Work. I never told my dad, he found out my senior year.

I've worked for several companies, from retail and customer service to one of the largest insurance companies in the country. Even at those jobs, I excelled because of my love for people, not because I folded shirts the best. However, I knew there was no way I could stay there for the rest of my life. Trust me, I get it, you gotta eat and those bills gotta get paid. As ideal as it would be, your purpose and career won't always coincide. I just want to make clear that it is never too late to begin the life that fulfills you the most, even if it is before or after you clock out. Ask yourself what you enjoy doing the most, and how you can incorporate that into your life for the betterment of you and anything outside of yourself. No matter how ridiculous you think it might be, this is YOUR gift to the world, that no one else can execute like you.

As jaded as being a social worker can make even the strongest person, no matter what new family is brought into my life, my intentions are always to make us both better in the end. Although traditional social work may not be my end goal, working socially will be my goal forever. I am blessed to know that I have found my purpose in helping others make their stories make sense, all while they are helping me make sense of mine. If I transition to my next life knowing I inspired at least one person to do the same, I'll leave with a completed mission.

No matter the circumstances, you were not brought into this world by mistake. You were chosen, and you are here to serve a purpose. You are capable of so much more than you can imagine, and it's never too late to find your purpose because your life is on no one's time but its own.

My prayer for every single person that is reading this as well as every single person that is not, is that you find your unique contribution that makes this world better, continue to bless us all with it, and strive to inspire someone else to do the same.

Reflection: Who inspires you, and why? What do you enjoy doing that gives you the most fulfillment? How can you use that to inspire others to do what fulfills them?

CHAPTER 7

"You wanna fly, you got to give up the thing that weighs
you down."—Toni Morrison

Heal

Let's heal!

I have spoken continuously about the work that I have
done and still have to do in order to at minimum main-
tain, but ideally progress, my Self. If you don't remember
anything in this book besides this chapter, I promise I will
be perfectly okay with that. Healing is the beginning of
every new journey. Just like you, an injury goes through
stages of healing before rehabilitating and being able to
operate at its full potential. Progress can be a slow process,
but evolution isn't instant. If you can show me a man that
does not evolve, I'll show you a dead man.

Therapy can be many things, but I highly recom-
mend that everyone speaks to a professional sometime in
their life. This is not to give up any therapeutic hobbies

already in place, but working out nonstop could be posing as a band-aid to the real issues at hand. I also want to make clear that every therapist is not for every client. Like any relationship, you can be incompatible with a therapist. Do not let a bad experience with one therapist ruin your outlook of them all. Also, be receptive to a perspective outside of your own, and do not enter a session only to be guarded and defensive. Be open, and more importantly, be honest—you owe it to yourself.

An ancient healing practice that I am fairly new to is holistic healing. Holistic healing focuses on the whole person, including the body, mind, spirit, and emotions. I know this particular practice isn't for everyone, but I strongly encourage you to research different holistic methods of healing.[4]

Smudging is a form of holistic healing that has become one of my favorite healing practices. Smudging is traditionally a ceremony for purifying or cleansing the soul of a person or place of negative thoughts. When a room or place is being smudged, the smoke is directed around the location, while the person conducting the ceremony prays for the negative energy to leave, and for positive energy to remain.[5] The ashes of the burned medicinal herbs are not discarded in a typical garbage receptacle;

---

4 https://www.webmd.com/balance/guide/what-is-holistic-medicine
5 https://www.ictinc.ca/blog/a-definition-of-smudging

rather, they are put outside, onto the earth, to signify that negative energy is placed outside of our lives.[6]

Whatever you choose to incorporate in your healing journey, always make sure you state your intention. Say a prayer, a mantra, or claim in advance what you're looking to manifest into your life. For example, while I am smudging, I'll repeat, "I speak favor over my life, peace of mind over my days, and peace and healing over my heart." Speak your future into existence and claim it as done.

I found that taking these four steps will help you tremendously in your journey:

Step 1: Forgive

Forgive your past. It's gone, and nothing and no one can change what has already happened. Forgive the things that were out of your control. Forgive the people who hurt you and understand that it had nothing to do with you, but everything to do with them. Forgive yourself for rushing your process and not trusting your journey.

Step 2: Give Love

Never get it confused, Love is the most powerful thing this world has to offer. When you act out of love, you act genuinely. When you are genuine, no matter the outcome, you're entitled to contentment. Whenever you're

---

6 https://www.thecanadianencyclopedia.ca/en/article/smudging

not doing something out of love, you're acting out of fear, and when you act with good intentions, there is no reason for you to be fearful of anything. Whatever is for you, will always be for you.

Step 3: Show Gratitude

There are endless reasons to be thankful. When you submit to life, you submit to the fact that you don't always know what's in your best interest. Your life passed on many things because they did not align with your future. Trust the timing and the process. Master the act of gratitude by being just as thankful for the things that did not happen as you are for the things that did.

Step 4: Inspire

If you follow the first three steps, this step is effortless. Never be ashamed to tell your story, especially when you're the only person who can tell it your way. You never know who you can help in the process. One of Mahatma Gandhi's most popular quotes is, "Be the change you want to see in the world." Aspire to inspire someone else to walk in their purpose as you execute walking in yours.

Healing is a process, and there will be times where triggers will cause you to react out of emotion. We are human, and sometimes emotions naturally overpower our logic. We can be hard on ourselves for making decisions that did not ideally go as planned. Healing is not instant, and never hesitate to repeat those steps as many times in your life as necessary. If you ever find yourself not feeling centered, gracefully start back at Step 1.

Reflection: Are you holding onto something you need to let go of? If so, what is it? Do you prioritize your self-care? What can you do at least once a week for self-care?

EPILOGUE

My dad's funeral was tough. I had so many unanswered questions, and so many apologies that I wanted to give him. Listening to everyone speak, I realized that no one knew him like I did; from his love for talk radio to his prejudice for lotion. When I spoke so intimately of him, it brought a lot of people to tears. After the service was over, several strangers came up to me with their condolences, telling me how much my dad talked about me, how my pictures were all over his office at work, and how I made him so proud. Life does not always give you what you want when you want it, but it does give you what you need when it's time.

If you ever need a refresher, just remember the following:

1. Trust your process

2. Treat your Trauma

3. Be conscious of who you allow in your space, and protect your energy at all costs

4. Be your own biggest advocate

5. Do not fear change

6. Find what fulfills you, and live in your purpose

7. HEAL by forgiving, loving, being grateful, and inspiring someone else to do the same

8. Self-reflect

We made it! That wasn't so bad, right?

Thank you, thank you, and thank you again. I am so overly humbled that you not only read this, but you finished it! I really hope you took the time to complete the reflection activities, as they are vital steps in beginning your healing. If not, you can always come back to them when you're ready. I love you solely for trusting me enough, allowing me to help you, and including me in this part of your journey.

Remember, there's no blueprint to this thing called life. We can watch, listen, and learn, but we cannot control anything but how we choose to move forward. I mentioned earlier on, that I did not have it all figured out. But maybe life isn't to be figured out, maybe it's just to be lived.

Did that make sense?

RESOURCES

Child Abuse or Neglect

If you suspect any child abuse or neglect, please call your local child protective services or law enforcement agency.

Childhelp National Child Abuse Hotline
1.800.4.A.CHILD (1.800.422.4453)

Public Assistance

Check with your local Department of Social Services for resources regarding food, healthcare, financial assistance, housing, and/or transportation.

USA.gov or call 1.844.USAGOV1 (1.844.872.4681) to ask for the information to your local Social Services agency.

Therapy

Ask your healthcare provider or primary care physician for mental health referrals covered under your health-care plan.

Search for a Therapist online:

Therapyforblackgirls.com

BEAM.community

TalkSpace

PsychologyToday.com

GoodTherapy.org

Findatherapist.com

Betterhelp.com

Faithfulcounseling.com

Also, search "Mindfulness" on your smartphone in your App Store for different wellness apps to find some that fit your personal preference.

WHO IS ERIN BATTLE?

Erin Battle grew up in Inglewood, Ca, and graduated from California State University, Los Angeles with a Bachelors of Arts in Social Work. She is a Children and Family Social Worker, and mother of one, trying to save the world, one person at a time. She is here to help you realize that life doesn't come with directions, so if you take a wrong turn, you can still make it to your destination. She's really just your homegirl rooting for you from a distance. You got this!